ideals® EASTER

Oh, happy, blessed Easter morn,
Oh, day of faith and hope reborn,
How bright the day, how warm the sun
To cheer the hearts of everyone!
—KATHLEEN R. PAWLEY

IDEALS PUBLICATIONS

NASHVILLE, TENNESSEE

In March

Beverly McLoughland

The garden is brown;
The garden is bare;
Winter bellows
A double-dare
At Spring, who boldly,
Despite the chill,
Smacks the Big Bully
With a daffodil.

When

Dorothy Aldis

In February there are days,
Blue, and nearly warm,
When horses switch their tails
     and ducks
Go quacking through the farm;
When everything turns round
     to full,
The sun upon its back—
When winter lifts a little bit,
And spring peeks through the crack.

Daffodils and flowering trees in Summit, New Jersey.
Photograph © Gene Ahrens/SuperStock

Spring
William D. Hicks

February rains down;
winter dreams of spring.
Clouds, fancy and full,
dance across windowpanes,
smeared icy clear.

A light, airy
cotton-candy world
loses its downy undercoat
of dreary white.
The sun ignites
the wick of the land.

Fragrant lilacs blossom
into lavender storybook paintings.
Vibrant fairy tale flowers
set amid a world afire.

Even in the Rain, the Birds Sing
Clay Harrison

Even in the rain the birds sing their songs of joy and praise,
For somehow they seem to know there will be brighter days.
Although the day grows dreary, sweet birdsong fills the air;
For it seems the April showers are answers to a prayer.
For my eyes have seen the glory of resurrected trees
When troubles seem to melt away in moments such as these.
Without the rain there'd be no hope for flowers in the spring;
So, like the birds, I learned to cope and let my glad heart sing.
Perhaps there will be rainbows when all is said and done.
For now, I'll sip a cup of tea and await the sleeping sun.

Tulips in a spring rain. Photograph © Rodho/Dreamstime.com

Spring Cleaning

Joan Donaldson

Every year, the sounds of spring ripple across our farm beginning with the first "Konk-la-ree" of the redwing blackbird, to the cheeping of peepers, and especially the bleating of baby goats. On a mild March evening, I opened the barn door and heard that long-awaited cry. Our trio of French Alpine goats had grown rounder and rounder until they preferred lounging in a scrap of sunshine instead of cavorting. My husband, John, and I had cleaned out the barn a couple of days ago in order to prepare for kidding season.

I knelt down on the fresh oat straw as Sallie licked the kid, cleaning and massaging his black-and-white body with her tongue. He chirped, and she rumbled with pleasure. Although only minutes old, he lifted his five-pound body, wobbled, and fell over. His resolve amazed me when he shook himself and struggled again to rise. I knew that hunger motivated him; but when facing challenges, how often do I show such persistence?

Sallie backed away and sank down. While I have assisted in a few difficult kiddings, most resembled her quick labor.

"You're doing fine," I said and stroked her side. "Baby number two is almost here."

Minnie and Betsy, our other goats, called out encouragment from beyond a gate that divided the stall illuminated by a row of windows. Our barn cats, Gracie and Spencer, sat on the manger, anticipating the time when the milk bucket would appear. And from their pen, our oxen, Buck and Henry, strained their necks, trying to view the maternity ward. No matter how large or small, our animals sense when something important is happening and want to share the event. Sometimes, they even solve a problem, such as when years ago, a single baby goat was born on a drizzly, cool day. I tried to wrap the baby in a towel, but she and her mama refused my blanket. Later, I found our calico cat cuddled with the kid. Kitty opened one eye and looked at me as if to say, "I have everything under control."

I forgot about the other animals while checking on baby number two and helping the kids find their way to Sallie's udder. Their tails wagged as they nursed. John entered the barn and offered a bucket of warm water sweetened with molasses to Sallie, who drank deeply.

"When you didn't return to the house, I figured Sallie was kidding. What are those oxen doing?"

Buck and Henry stood outside, licking the windows, removing the winter grime. Their chestnut eyes gazed down at the young kids.

"They couldn't see from their stall, so they figured out how to look in," I said.

John laughed and went to give them apples. But the oxen's efforts had reminded me of the need to spring-clean my home. Tomorrow, I would wash my windows, welcoming in sunshine and a better view of baby goats gamboling in their pasture.

*He sendeth the springs
into the valleys,
which run among the hills.*
—Psalm 104:10

An Easter Storm

Gail L. Roberson

I love a spring storm; I am usually somewhere in the middle of its whirling metallic sheets of pelting rain. One Easter weekend, however, we had a full-blown, raging wind- and rainstorm that lifted the tops off of some of the farm shelters and uprooted trees. In the county next door, a tornado had touched down; and we had received a lot of its wind. Luckily, no one had been hurt. As the men began repairs and women set pots to boil, I made it my business to confer with Mother Nature. It didn't take me long to note that, from out of the damage just done, there was already a resurrection taking place. New piglets had been born during the storm, as had a calf whose mother was licking it dry even as I found it.

The water was high in the creek and ditches, and a variety of wildlife had come to drink. Wiggling, elastic-like earthworms had fled their burrows and were being scooped up heartily by varieties of birds come to take advantage, while the tiny flowers along the paths that were not open yesterday were now in full bloom. The storm had brought much damage, but it could not stop Easter. The colors, aromas, and new birth that are symbols of the season continued despite fallen, crisscrossed trees and shingles blown for miles. Even before my cousin uprighted the rockers on her porch, she went to the church to make certain the offering table was ready for service in the morning.

I happened upon bark flung far from the tree and started looking upward, following the scent of fresh resin until I found the pine whose top had been blown apart by a bolt from the blue. With great gusto, a commotion of woodpeckers had taken charge of the termites now exposed in their nest. Wasps, hornets, and bumblebees were working on new hives and were now wet and grumpy, their own homes having suffered damage as well. I noted that the resurrection ferns lining one tree's limb were no longer crispy and dry, but had pumped themselves up with water and were now thick, green, and lush. How appropriate for this weekend in particular.

What had died would be reborn again in a new generation of seed, egg, root, or an offering as sustenance for some other living thing. Such is the circle and the cycle of life. Something has to die in order for something else to live.

That Easter Sunday, the service was much longer than usual. The women knew it would be, and prepared their meals accordingly. Much prayer was lifted up for those who had suffered, much thanks for those who had not, and many plans made for the day afterwards when everyone would come together in renewed friendship and hope to help their neighbors rebuild and repair after the Easter storm.

A flowering redbud against the Merced River in the Sierra National Forest, California. Photograph © Terry Donnelly/Donnelly-Austin Photography

Bits & Pieces

I think of the garden after the rain,
And hope to my heart comes singing,
"At morn the cherry-blooms will be white,
And the Easter bells be ringing!"
—*Edna Dean Procter*

The glittering drops come dashing by,
Eager to leave the restless sky,
And drop on the old earth's welcoming lap,
As the flowers awake from their winter nap.
—*Martha Hood*

Rain! whose soft architectural hands have
power to cut stones and chisel to shapes of
grandeur the very mountains.
—*Henry Ward Beecher*

I saw God wash the world last night
With His sweet showers on high,
And then when morning came,
I saw Him hang it out to dry.
—*William L. Stidger*

Like a cooling kiss from heaven, a sweet, descending shower
Falls gently on the buds of bush and tree and flower.
It bids them to awaken and blossom forth again,
As Spring in all her splendor comes tripping down the lane.
—*LaVerne P. Larson*

Rain is grace; rain is the
sky condescending to the
earth; without rain, there
would be no life.
—*John Updike*

The best thing one can
do when it's raining is
to let it rain.
—*Henry Wadsworth Longfellow*

Sweet April showers
do spring May flowers.
—*Thomas Tusser*

Cherry Blossom Pond

N. Anne Highlands Tiley

The wind is in the willows
Steering petal blossom islands
Where the clusters of pink cherry blooms
Are congregate on idles of the rippling pond.
The tree that set a garden's hues
Upwards toward the sky as if
Its branches formed horizons, no need to look beyond,
Is now greening since a blush has settled on the pond.
And in the tender, nearly leafing woodland,
Where spring is all but just begun,
Silene caroliniana raises pink islands from the ground—
Terrestrial islands moored in root and stem
And passengered by lady bugs with a restive wing.

Easter's Coming!

Aileen Fisher

Through the sunshine,
through the shadow,
down the hillside,
down the meadow,
little streams run bright and merry,
bursting with the news they carry,
singing, shouting,
laughing, humming,
"Easter's coming,
Easter's coming!"

Photograph © OGphoto/iStockphoto

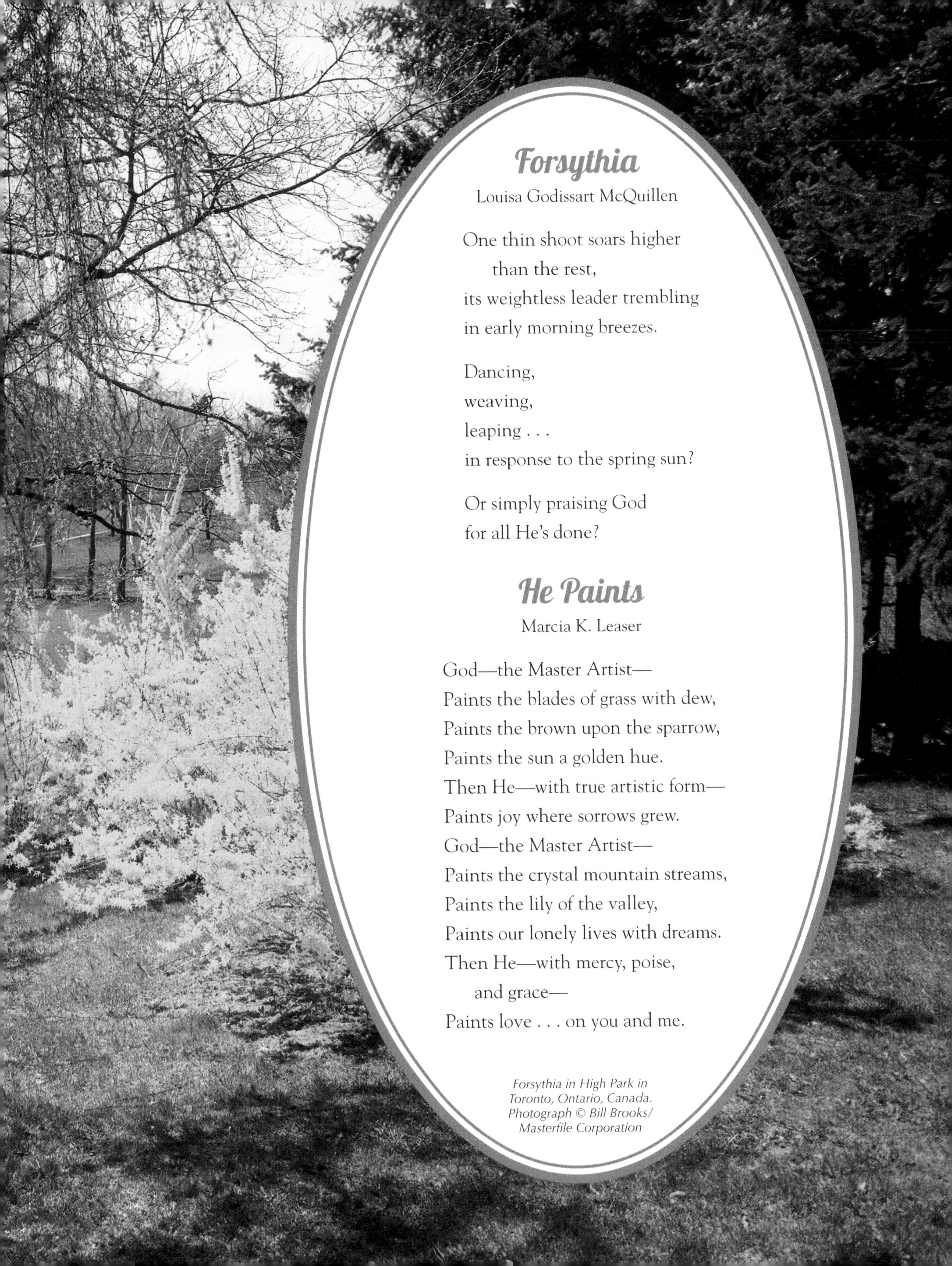

Forsythia

Louisa Godissart McQuillen

One thin shoot soars higher
    than the rest,
its weightless leader trembling
in early morning breezes.

Dancing,
weaving,
leaping . . .
in response to the spring sun?

Or simply praising God
for all He's done?

He Paints

Marcia K. Leaser

God—the Master Artist—
Paints the blades of grass with dew,
Paints the brown upon the sparrow,
Paints the sun a golden hue.
Then He—with true artistic form—
Paints joy where sorrows grew.
God—the Master Artist—
Paints the crystal mountain streams,
Paints the lily of the valley,
Paints our lonely lives with dreams.
Then He—with mercy, poise,
    and grace—
Paints love . . . on you and me.

*Forsythia in High Park in
Toronto, Ontario, Canada.
Photograph © Bill Brooks/
Masterfile Corporation*

The Buds of Spring

Gerry Childs

Spring has turned the corner, and it is pleasant these days to walk in a warming woodland while the sun's rays paint pictures on the faded leaf carpet. The muted brown and yellow, bronze and gray, are reminiscent of an antique, soft-hued Oriental rug.

Beneath the moist carpet, the magic of life is stirring in the black, primal humus on which all life depends. Interlocked branches above form the cathedral aisles of a woodland sanctuary.

While the woodland warms and the floor is soft and moist, buds are starting to swell and soon will part the scales in which miniatures leaves and blossoms were wrapped last summer.

There is heart-lift in the woodland on a warm, breezeless day. Chickadees sing their two-toned song. The robins have arrived, and their cheery morning songs greet us from meadow and lawn. The tapping of a woodpecker on a resonant dead limb accentuates the peacefulness. There is a satisfying, heady fragrance from the warming leaf mold.

Each person has his favorite sign of spring. There are those who think that on a sunny, fourth-month day, when white clouds dot the sky and the tones of the village bell float by on the golden air, that a warming woodland is the most certain omen of the great turn.

No man need be lonely in this experience of time if trees are his friends. Steadfast through the years, they turn to green bouquets in spring.

Now we're on the threshold of one of nature's most exciting, inspiring times. The buds of spring are starting to show the renewal of life.

When a winter of tempest and snow is done, the life juices climb again to the farthermost twig and bud. A man walking his woodland on a pleasant day can feel a faith that gives meaning to life.

Carpet of bluebells. Photograph © Adifor/Dreamstime.com

Spring
Ethel Wilson

The shades of Spring are here again;
Red Robin's bared his breast;
the blue, blue bluejay flying by
has built himself a nest;
the green, green grass is peeping out
from 'neath the brown, brown earth;
and all the world's been waiting for
these signs of Spring—new birth!
The crocus and the daffodil,
forsythia and trees
are pushing forth their little buds,
warmed by the wafting breeze.
Purple lilacs, violets blue,
tulips of every hue
announce that Spring has finally come,
and all her clothes are new!

Harbingers of Spring
Virginia Blanck Moore

Open the windows
and open the door.
The lilacs are blooming;
and also, what's more,
the neighbors are cutting
their lawns and oh, my,
how sweet are the breezes
that go drifting by!

You can't smell the rhubarb,
but it's fast growing high,
and we're just days away
from the aroma of pie.
We don't need a date book
or any such thing—
the heavenly scents
enveloping us
all say, "It's spring!"

Photograph © Liliya Kulianionak/Shutterstock

Easter in Our Village

Earle J. Grant

Easter in our village
Is a lovely time,
With snowy lilies,
Church bells' chimes;
Easter in our village
Means egg-hunt thrills,
Downy bunnies,
   new clothes,
Dogwoods frosting hills.

Easter in our village
Means greening awards
And the shops featuring
Lovely greeting cards
That proclaim once more
The immortal Story
That the Tomb is empty
And Christ reigns in Glory!

Joyous Easter Season

Alice M. Stewart

Joyous Easter season,
Resurrection time:
Pealing from church steeples
Hear the glad bells chime!
They ring out the story
Of the empty tomb.
Listen to their harmony
Dispersing winter's gloom.

Joyous Easter season,
Most blessed of the year.
Hear the choirs singing,
Voices pure and clear.

Hymn and anthem offer
Praise to Christ above,
Who gave His life for others . . .
A sacrifice of love.

Joyous Easter season:
See the blossoms bright
Lift their smiling faces
Upward to the light,
Looking to the sunshine,
Knowing well it's true
Springtime and Eastertime
Wake the Earth anew.

Spring Is Coming

Jane McGuire Reneau

When summer begins to come to a close and the weather starts to finally cool off, I am always so ready. I am usually tired of the oppressive heat, ready to run in cooler temperatures, ready for mittens, scarves, and hats. I am ready to build fires in the fireplace and to see my breath in the brisk night air.

With the close of winter and the rise of temperatures, however, I am equally ready. I am ready for my skin to breathe in the fresh morning air. I am ready to feel the sun on my shoulders. I am ready to replace my mittens, scarves, and hats with tank tops, flip-flops, and dinner on the back porch.

That is where I find myself today. It seems the last vestiges of winter are holding on with both hands as we enjoy a warm Sunday afternoon and then a frigid Monday morning. The sunshine teases me into believing spring is here, but the cold winds continue to blow. Even so, flowers are beginning to bloom. Trees are slowly turning green. Instead of bare trees against a gray sky, color begins to appear here and there. The sound of lawn mowers fills the afternoon air; and more people are seen walking dogs, pushing strollers, and jogging down my neighborhood streets.

This is what I love about spring. It isn't just that I can shed my thick winter sweaters, and all the layers I wear when I am out running. It is also the feeling of waking up. It is the feeling of breathing a little deeper, of taking in the first scents of fresh air and being renewed. It is the feeling of life starting all over again. Maybe that is the origin of spring-cleaning—the desire to open windows, air out the closed-in spaces, letting in all that is new and fresh and pure. It is the desire to see things grow, to plant flowers in my yard and watch beauty explode all around me with the changing of the season. It gives me this brand-new feeling, making me want to have everything around me as fresh, clean, and new as the breeze outside.

With the coming of spring comes Easter as well. Another day of renewing, awakening life. Maybe it was the divine plan that we would celebrate the day our Savior rose from the dead as flowers are blooming, eggs are hatching, birdsong returns to the mornings, and everything seems to be coming to life once more.

So while the day outside is cold, gray, and rainy, I know it will not last. I know spring is coming; and no matter how the winds may blow, I know the flowers are lying in wait. I know there are leaves ready to sprout and baby birds ready to grow and sing; I know sunshine will be there when the cold winds subside. Just like I know when things get difficult and life seems to be no good at all, there is a Man who came to this earth to give life. He came to make new all that was old, weary, gray, and cold. He overcame all that was bad in this world, even death.

That, to me, is the most wonderful reason of all to celebrate the season.

Featured Poet

Egg Hunt

Eileen Spinelli

Distracted from the path
I see
a twinkling creek.
It splashes me.

What flower this?
What swooning scent?
Here willow makes
a feathered tent.

There sunlight speckles
dancing bees.
I learn the hum of
April's breeze.

Then—time is up.
Egg hunt is done.
Eggs are counted
one by one.

My pail is empty—
not a thing . . .
but, oh, my heart
is filled
with spring.

Easter Is a Constant Spring

Ruth Carrington

Easter is a reminding time:
Of colored eggs and
    pretty dresses;
Of yellow chicks and
    curly tresses.

Easter is a renewing time:
For baby bunnies, birds,
    and bees;
For sun and rain on
    budding trees.

Easter is a grateful time:
For all our blessings every day;
For health and friends
    along the way.

Easter is a believing time:
That Christ arose for us to see
The way to grow eternally.

Easter is a joyful time:
For thoughts, for growth,
    for songs to sing.
Yes, Easter is a constant spring.

Easter

Irene Randol

When we're youngsters, Easter's dandy:
colored eggs, new toys, and candy;
Easter bunnies and chickens too;
Easter outfits, all bright and new;
Easter bonnets, all frills and lace;
a sunny smile on each small face;
the many joys that come with spring,
birds and flowers and everything.
But then it isn't long before
we realize that it means much more—
how Jesus rose upon that day
(He'd died to wash our sins away).
So when Eastertime is here,
we raise our voices loud and clear;
praise His name to Heaven above,
rejoicing in so great a love!
So whether we be man or boy,
Easter is a time of joy.

The Hunt-Helper

Conny Manero

Easter Sunday celebrates the Resurrection of Jesus; but for children the world over, Easter means a celebration of chocolate—chocolate eggs, chocolate bunnies, and a variety of other candy.

While in some places it is the Easter Bunny that drops off chocolate eggs and bunnies for children, in parts of Europe, children believe the bells of Rome knock the tasty treats into their backyard.

As a child I didn't doubt this story for a moment. On Easter morning, I stood in my pajamas in front of the living-room window, facing the garden, trying to spot the white and light and dark brown eggs and bunnies, to get there ahead of my seven-years-older brother. My brother played along to humor me. Such fun I had, looking for the eggs, dashing from one place to another, filling my basket with eggs and bunnies of various sizes.

Every year there was also one very large egg, stuffed with pralines, wrapped in see-through foil, held together with a red silk ribbon. It was understood that the bells of Rome had dropped off this particular egg for my mother.

Once I was a mother myself, I carried on the tradition of a chocolate-egg hunt with my son. While my husband kept five-year-old Dieter indoors and entertained him, I hid the eggs in the garden, seeking out shadowed places. Somewhere along the line I was joined by Mickey, our seven-year-old tabby cat. He trotted alongside with me as I placed egg after egg under bushes and trees.

Once I was finished, I called to my son that the Easter Bunny had been here, that he could—

Before the sentence was finished, Dieter flew into the hall and out the door.

He found five of the fifteen eggs in under a minute, but then he came to a standstill—where to look next?

Mickey, who was sitting some distance away, turned his head towards my son and let out a loud *meow*. Dieter looked up, saw Mickey near a rosebush, and spotted the sixth egg.

Once the egg was found, Mickey moved to a nearby palm and let out another meow. Dieter followed.

The rest of the egg hunt proceeded in similar fashion. Some eggs and bunnies Dieter found without assistance; and at times when he got stuck, all he had to do was look for the cat.

Needless to say, the following year while I was hiding the eggs, Mickey was kept indoors.

ANNIE ON THE GOLDEN WALL *by Susan Bourdet. Artwork courtesy of the artist and Wild Wings (800-445-4833; www.wildwings.com)*

The Annual Easter Eggstravaganza

Michelle Medlock Adams

My mom, or Mamaw, loved planning elaborate family events such as "The Medlock Easter Egg Eggstravaganza." Shopping weeks in advance of Easter, she would find every grandchild's favorite candy and several special trinkets and toys that she could stuff into each of the pastel-colored plastic eggs. My Dad, or Papaw, liked to get in on the Easter Egg Eggstravaganza too, so he stuffed money into several of the eggs—a few had ten- or five-dollar bills, but most contained one-dollar bills or quarters. Mamaw and Papaw would then hide the carefully prepared eggs throughout their yard. They hid the eggs under the sundeck, in flowerpots, and even in the mailbox. They loved this process, acting almost as giddy as the grandkids who would soon find the treasure-filled eggs.

Mamaw and Papaw had a system to ensure every grandchild received the same amount of candy, toys, and money: they labeled each egg with a name. The kids were allowed to help one another find their designated eggs, but they could not take each other's eggs. So if Ally found Abby's egg, she would have to put it back where she found it and go in search of her own eggs. It made for a fun afternoon of searching and helping and finding and giggling and celebrating.

It was the most anticipated event in our family—a Medlock family tradition. As much as our girls loved hunting for Easter eggs in Mamaw and Papaw's yard, we figured they'd also love the large community egg hunt, so we took them one year. But as Abby ran from hiding spot to hiding spot, she was outmaneuvered by various faster, older children, who would snatch the brightly colored plastic eggs before Abby could grab each one. This happened to Abby and Ally over and over again as they braved the bigger kids in search of their very own Easter egg.

My husband and I were enjoying the beautiful weather, chatting with a few other parents from our neighborhood, when we heard cries of desperation from Abby, followed by gasps and sobs coming from Ally. When I found our girls, they were sitting down next to their empty Easter baskets, totally tuckered out and troubled from the unsuccessful hunt. That was the moment it dawned on me that they'd never been to an actual Easter egg hunt! At Mamaw Medlock's Easter Egg Eggstravaganza, there was no panic, no fighting, no stress, and no disappointment. They didn't have to sweat the hunt because they knew there would be eggs with their names on them just waiting to be found. The girls had looked forward to this citywide Easter egg hunt, but they were no longer in good spirits.

Through tears, Abby whimpered, "The big kids took all the eggs, Mommy!"

Ally, who had found a roly-poly bug in the dirt to entertain her, had tear-stained cheeks and a quivering bottom lip. She was too upset to talk. As Daddy grabbed their empty Easter baskets, I took their hands and we all headed to our car. As I used wet wipes to remove the roly-poly germs and dirt from the girls' faces, I tried to explain to the girls how actual Easter egg hunts work and how Mamaw and Papaw's Easter Egg Eggstravaganza was a "fixed" egg hunt. Abby looked up at me with her big green eyes and said, "Mommy, we liked fixed ones best." Ally nodded in agreement.

I'm with Abby and Ally. I liked fixed Easter egg hunts best too. That's why I love walking with the Lord every single day—not just on Easter—because He orchestrates my life in such a way that I feel as if I'm living out the joy, excitement, and celebration of a fixed Easter egg hunt. When I open up His Word and search the Scriptures,

I find promises with my name on them, full of treasure just for me. When I read Jeremiah 29:11, which says that He has a good plan for me, I can smile and say, "Yes!" and put that promise in the "basket" otherwise known as my heart. Looking back on the love, enthusiasm, and care that my parents put into each Easter egg hunt, I remember that my Heavenly Father is even more loving, enthusiastic, and caring when it comes to His children. He has many treasures stored up for us—that's what His Word says—and I believe it because my "basket" is full today. If you find that yours feels empty this season, go on a hunt through God's Word and begin filling your heart with His promises. This life is "fixed" in our favor by a loving God. No matter how many people push us out of the way and steal what we had our eyes on, God has good things awaiting us. Happy Resurrection Day, and happy hunting!

Sabbath of the Palm

Edgar A. Guest

This the Sabbath of the palm,
This His last of holy days,
This the glory and the calm
Ere the storm which fear should raise!

This the day disciples heard,
"Go to where a colt is tied,
If they question say the word,
'Tis the Lord who comes to ride."

As He neared, the happy throng
Spread their garments in His way
And, with waving palm and song,
Greeted Him this Sabbath day.

Soon should terror-stricken power
Vinegar His cup of balm—
This His last triumphant hour,
Called the Sabbath of the palm.

Palm Sunday

Laurie E. Dawson

I would have liked to walk along the way,
And wave the branches green and gay;
To have caught a glimpse of the gentle face
As He rode that day with lowly grace.

I wish I could have sung His praise
And known about His kingly ways;
To have seen the love upon His face,
As He rode that day with measured pace.

I was not there, but still I know
The many ways that I can show
My love for others and keep today,
Palm Sunday, in my heart to stay.

*Palm tree in front of Waiʻoli Huiʻia Church, Kauai,
Hawaii. Photograph © Don White/SuperStock*

Easter Lily

Diane Skinner

"Consider the lilies, how they grow."
—Luke 12:27a (RSV)

Powder-white petals began to unfold as our lily bathed in sunlight. It seemed as if the bulb's autumn planting had been only yesterday; yet, now saturated with sunshine, its barren appearance was clothed with new life. Hopefully by the morning of Easter, it would become a cluster of blooms.

Filling the sprinkling can to water the plant, I marveled at the delicate lily, God's age-old creation and symbol of beauty. How often our Lord trekked through the Judean hills and breathlessly gazed at its petals as they rippled in glory.

'Tis no wonder He left behind the simple command, "Consider the lilies."

Digging out last year's baskets and making mental notes to buy eggs, dye, and grass, I could not escape thoughts of my lily and the Lord's admonition: "Consider . . . how they grow." Buried below the sod, its seed emerges triumphant, alive, and garnished in white. Surely this lovely plant symbolizes the Savior's three-day descent into the pit of the earth, only to rise above death, fully resurrected, and glowing in white.

Planning to buy straw hats and shoes for my girls, I thought of my mother and the Easters we'd spent. Oh, how I missed her! Perhaps she too was preparing for Lent from heaven's portals in her garments of white. Somehow I could rejoice in the midst of my grief, knowing that someday I'd see her again. I had my Father's Word: whoever "believes in me shall not die." (John 11:26b, RSV) and again "In my Father's house are many rooms; if it were not so, would I have told you that I go to prepare a place for you?" (John 14:2).

As I hastily scribbled down additional items needed for the day's feast—ham basted in pineapple, candied yams, hot cross buns with mint jelly, lime salad, fruit pies, and chocolate eggs— I was eager to plan my day. Outward festivities played an important part of this year's holiday, but as I cast one more glance at the sunlight fading upon my lily, I had ultimately discovered the real and deeper meaning that Easter brings. Man, like the lily, "does not come to life unless it dies" (1 Corinthians 15:36b). Yes, I had surrendered my life to God and become a new creation in Him; and because of this miracle born of Easter, I knew someday I too would be resurrected, living, and dazzling in white!

A Hymn to the Good Father

Ben Jonson

Hear me, O God!
A broken heart
Is my best part:
Use still Thy rod,
That I may prove,
Therein, Thy love.

If Thou hadst not
Been stern to me,
But left me free,
I had forgot
Myself and Thee.

For sin's so sweet,
As minds ill bent
Rarely repent
Until they meet
Their punishment.

Who more can crave
Than Thou hast done:
That gav'st a Son
To free a slave?
First made of nought,
Withal since bought.

Sin, death, and hell
His glorious Name
Quite overcame,
Yet I rebel
And slight the same.

But I'll come in
Before my loss
Me farther toss,
As sure to win
Under His cross.

View of sunset over Mackinac Island Harbor, Michigan.
Photograph by John McCormick/michigannut/Dreamstime.com

The Sunbeam in the Shadows

Pamela Kennedy

At Easter, many of us think of light: the brilliance of the rising sun or the blinding brightness of the angelic messenger telling Mary, "He is not here, He is risen!" But preceding the sunshine of Easter, the cross cast its long shadow on that first Good Friday. Almost two millennia later, a young Scottish woman's poem captured the central irony of that first Easter—the sorrow that led to victory, the shadows that made way for the sun.

One of three daughters born to the county sheriff of Melrose, Scotland, Elizabeth Cecilia Douglas Clephane experienced a challenging childhood. Not only did she suffer from frequent illnesses, but she also endured great emotional loss when both of her parents died. Elizabeth immersed herself in literature and the Scriptures and discovered solace in writing spiritual poetry. By her late teens, Elizabeth had turned her personal pain into a commitment to serve others. She took Christ's words in Matthew 16:24 as her credo: "Whoever will come after me, let him deny himself and take up his cross and follow me." Elizabeth sold most of her belongings and used the proceeds to purchase food and clothing for the poor and sick in her community. Then, despite her own physical weak-ness, she spent hours each day serving others, sharing with them her worldly goods as well as her belief that God saw and cared for their needs. Her cheerful demeanor and encouraging words earned her the nickname "The Sunbeam," as she carried the light of Christ into every home she visited.

Elizabeth Clephane also continued to compose poetry centered upon religious themes, many of which were published anonymously in the Scottish Presbyterian magazine, *The Family Treasury*. Shortly after her death at the age of thirty-nine, however, a collection of her poetry was compiled and published under her name. The British organist Frederick Charles Maker received a copy of the small book and created a melody for the words to one of Elizabeth's poems, "Beneath the Cross of Jesus."

In the three verses of this lovely hymn, both the intellect and faith of its author shine through in the images of shadow and sunlight. In the powerful third verse, the young woman known as "The Sunbeam" expresses her desire to remain forever in the shadow of the cross, basking there in the sunshine of Christ's face. By earthly standards, Elizabeth Clephane may have lived a short life filled with dark moments, but the words of her lovely hymn invite those willing to enjoy the healing light and love she discovered "beneath the cross of Jesus."

"Beneath the Cross of Jesus"

by Elizabeth Clephane, music by Frederick C. Maker

1. Be-neath the cross of Je - sus I fain would take my stand, The
2. Up-on that cross of Je - sus mine eye at times can see The
3. I take, O cross, thy shad - ow for my a - bid-ing place; I

shad - ow of a might - y rock with - in a wea - ry land; A
ver - y dy - ing form of One Who suf - fered there for me; And
ask no oth - er sun - shine than the sun - shine of His face; Con-

home with - in the wil - der - ness, a rest up - on the way, From the
from my smit-ten heart with tears two won - ders I con-fess; The
tent to let the world go by, to know no gain nor loss, My

burn - ing of the noon - tide heat, and the bur - den of the day.
won - ders of re - deem - ing love and my un - wor - thi - ness.
sin - ful self my on - ly shame, my glo - ry all the cross.

Good Friday

Sheila J. Petre

Perhaps that day was gauzed with mist.
Perhaps the air was light.
Perhaps the rain fell trembling down,
Before that Life took flight.
We know that for three lonely hours,
The day was stunned to night.

Perhaps the soul is clothed in gold.
Perhaps its veil is grief.
Perhaps its fog has lingered low,
Defying mind's belief.
Each heart must know its hour of dark
Before the Light's relief.

She Knew

Marcia K. Leaser

Mary knew who You were, Lord,
and yet she hid it in her heart.
She ran back to the temple
when she discovered You were gone.
And even though You were merely a child,
You were about Your Father's business.
How often did her heart ache,
as she watched the ones You loved
betray . . . deny . . . and crucify?
How could she bear the pain
and not feel anger toward them?
As from the cross, You forgave
The very ones who hung You there.
The answer lies plain before us—
It is because . . . she knew.

Photograph © prochasson frederic/Shutterstock

Borrowed

Author Unknown

They borrowed a bed to lay His head,
When Christ the Lord came down,
They borrowed a foal in the
    mountain pass
For Him to ride to town.
But the crown that He wore
And the cross that He bore
Were His own.

He borrowed the bread when the
    crowd He fed
On the grassy mountainside;
He borrowed the dish of
    broken fish
With which he satisified.
But the crown that He wore
And the cross that He bore
Were His own.

He borrowed the ship in which to sit
To teach the multitude;
He borrowed the nest in which
    to rest;
He had never a home as rude.

But the crown that He wore
And the cross that He bore
Were His own.

He borrowed a room on the way
    to the tomb,
The Passover lamb to eat.
They borrowed a cave,
    for Him a grave;
They borrowed a winding sheet.
But the crown that He wore
And the cross that He bore
Were His own.

The thorns on His head were worn
    in my stead—
For me the Savior died;
For guilt of my sin the nails
    drove in,
When Him they crucified.
Though the crown that He wore
And the cross that He bore
Were His own . . .
They rightly were mine, instead.

The Triumphal Entry

Mark 11:1–11a

And when they came nigh to Jerusalem, unto Bethphage and Bethany, at the mount of Olives, he sendeth forth two of his disciples, And saith unto them, Go your way into the village over against you: and as soon as ye be entered into it, ye shall find a colt tied, whereon never man sat; loose him, and bring him. And if any man say unto you, Why do ye this? say ye that the Lord hath need of him; and straightway he will send him hither.

And they went their way, and found the colt tied by the door without in a place where two ways met; and they loose him.

And certain of them that stood there said unto them, What do ye, loosing the colt?

And they said unto them even as Jesus had commanded: and they let them go.

And they brought the colt to Jesus, and cast their garments on him; and he sat upon him.

And many spread their garments in the way: and others cut down branches off the trees, and strawed them in the way.

And they that went before, and they that followed, cried, saying, Hosanna; Blessed is he that cometh in the name of the Lord:

Blessed be the kingdom of our father David, that cometh in the name of the Lord: Hosanna in the highest.

And Jesus entered into Jerusalem, and into the temple.

Truly the Son of God

Matthew 27:33–54

And when they were come unto a place called Golgotha, that is to say, a place of a skull, They gave him vinegar to drink mingled with gall: and when he had tasted thereof, he would not drink.

And they crucified him, and parted his garments, casting lots: that it might be fulfilled which was spoken by the prophet, They parted my garments among them, and upon my vesture did they cast lots. And sitting down they watched him there; And set up over his head his accusation written, THIS IS JESUS THE KING OF THE JEWS.

Then were there two thieves crucified with him, one on the right hand, and another on the left. And they that passed by reviled him, wagging their heads, And saying, Thou that destroyest the temple, and buildest it in three days, save thyself. If thou be the Son of God, come down from the cross.

Likewise also the chief priests mocking him, with the scribes and elders, said, He saved others; himself he cannot save. If he be the King of Israel, let him now come down from the cross, and we will believe him. He trusted in God; let him deliver him now, if he will have him: for he said, I am the Son of God. The thieves also, which were crucified with him, cast the same in his teeth.

Now from the sixth hour there was darkness over all the land unto the ninth hour. And about the ninth hour Jesus cried with a loud voice, saying, Eli, Eli, lama sabachthani? that is to say, My God, my God, why hast thou forsaken me?

Some of them that stood there, when they heard that, said, This man calleth for Elias. And straightway one of them ran, and took a spunge, and filled it with vinegar, and put it on a reed, and gave him to drink. The rest said, Let be, let us see whether Elias will come to save him.

Jesus, when he had cried again with a loud voice, yielded up the ghost.

And, behold, the veil of the temple was rent in twain from the top to the bottom; and the earth did quake, and the rocks rent; And the graves were opened; and many bodies of the saints which slept arose, And came out of the graves after his resurrection, and went into the holy city, and appeared unto many.

Now when the centurion, and they that were with him, watching Jesus, saw the earthquake, and those things that were done, they feared greatly, saying, Truly this was the Son of God.

Burial and Resurrection

Matthew 27:55–66, 28:1–8

And many women were there beholding afar off, which followed Jesus from Galilee, ministering unto him: Among which was Mary Magdalene, and Mary the mother of James and Joses, and the mother of Zebedee's children.

When the even was come, there came a rich man of Arimathaea, named Joseph, who also himself was Jesus' disciple: He went to Pilate, and begged the body of Jesus. Then Pilate commanded the body to be delivered. And when Joseph had taken the body, he wrapped it in a clean linen cloth, And laid it in his own new tomb, which he had hewn out in the rock: and he rolled a great stone to the door of the sepulchre, and departed. And there was Mary Magdalene, and the other Mary, sitting over against the sepulchre.

Now the next day, that followed the day of the preparation, the chief priests and Pharisees came together unto Pilate, Saying, Sir, we remember that that deceiver said, while he was yet alive, After three days I will rise again.

Command therefore that the sepulchre be made sure until the third day, lest his disciples come by night, and steal him away, and say unto the people, He is risen from the dead: so the last error shall be worse than the first. Pilate said unto them, Ye have a watch: go your way, make it as sure as ye can. So they went, and made the sepulchre sure, sealing the stone, and setting a watch.

In the end of the sabbath, as it began to dawn toward the first day of the week, came Mary Magdalene and the other Mary to see the sepulchre.

And, behold, there was a great earthquake: for the angel of the Lord descended from heaven, and came and rolled back the stone from the door, and sat upon it. His countenance was like lightning, and his raiment white as snow: And for fear of him the keepers did shake, and became as dead men.

And the angel answered and said unto the women, Fear not ye: for I know that ye seek Jesus, which was crucified. He is not here: for he is risen, as he said. Come, see the place where the Lord lay. And go quickly, and tell his disciples that he is risen from the dead; and, behold, he goeth before you into Galilee; there shall ye see him: lo, I have told you.

And they departed quickly from the sepulchre with fear and great joy; and did run to bring his disciples word.

Easter Message

Gladys Harp

Oh, glad triumphal Easter morning,
Such sweet relief its message gives;
Oh, come, behold the blest Redeemer!
He is not dead! He lives! He lives!

Satan's wiles with sin have bound us,
Hence we merit heaven's loss;

But the Son of God did free us
When He died upon the cross.

Oh, gracious promise to believers—
Because He died our souls to save,
We, on the resurrection morning,
Shall rise exultant from the grave!

Sunrise over the ocean in Pacific Grove, California. Photograph © Dennis Frates Photography

The Easter Message

Margaret Rorke

Of all the words that have been said
Throughout recorded time
The angel's news: "He is not dead!"
Is, doubtless, most sublime.
It underscores Christ's work and worth;
It proves His promise true
And offers hope to all on earth
Like nothing else can do.

Apostles bowed by loss and grief,
By shaken faith and fear,
Sought evidence before belief
Like many now and here.
He gave them proof—the proof we heed
On every Easter Day—
The proof Christ lives and is, indeed,
The Truth, the Life, the Way.

Tell Me the Old, Old Story

Katherine Hankey

Tell me the old, old story
Of unseen things above,
Of Jesus and His glory,
Of Jesus and His love.

Tell me the story simply,
As to a little child,
For I am weak and weary
And helpless and defiled.

Tell me the story slowly,
That I may take it in—
That wonderful redemption,
God's remedy for sin.
Tell me the story often,
For I forget so soon;
The early dew of morning
Has passed away at noon.

Tell me the story softly,
With earnest tones, and grave;
Remember! I'm a sinner
Whom Jesus came to save.
Tell me that story always,
If you would really be,
In any time of trouble,
A comforter to me.

Tell me the same old story
When you have cause to fear
That this world's empty glory
Is costing me too dear.
Yes, and when that world's glory
Is dawning on my soul,
Tell me the old, old story:
Christ Jesus makes me whole.

Unbounded Love

Susan Sundwall

As ripples of our Savior's death
were felt throughout the land,
the fate of all the living lay
in God's almighty hand.

Never was a man so good,
never one so mild.
His holy act of sacrifice
touched every earthly child.

His love did not know
    boundaries,
His mercies just and true,

His yoke and burden easy
and borne for me and you.

Lay at His feet your troubles
and yearning to believe,
for those who hold Him in
    their hearts
His promise will receive.

As ripples of our Savior's life
rise gently in our souls;
the glory of the Easter morn
has come to make us whole.

Daffodils near church in Hillsborough Center, New Hampshire. Photograph © William H. Johnson

Easter

John Banister Tabb

Like a meteor, large and bright,
Fell a golden seed of light
On the field of Christmas night
When the Babe was born.

Then 'twas sepulchred in gloom,
Till above His holy tomb
Flashed its everlasting bloom—
Flower of Easter morn!

The Revival

Henry Vaughan

Unfold, unfold! take in His light,
who makes thy cares more short
    than night.
The joys, with which His day-star rise,
He deals to all, but drowsy eyes:
And what the men of this world miss,
Some drops and dews of future bliss.
Hark! how His winds have changed
    their note,
And with warm whispers call thee out.
The frosts are past, the storms are gone:
And backward life at last comes on.
The lofty groves in express joys
Reply above the turtle's voice,
And here in dust and dirt, O here
The lilies of His love appear!

*Sunset at Obstruction Point in Olympic National
Park, Washington. Photograph © Rob Tilley/
DanitaDelimont.com*

Out of the Darkness
(Matthew 28:1–10)

Pamela Kennedy

"Savta! Savta!" Mary heard the child's cries and hurried to her bedside.

"What is it, Sarah?" she asked, gathering her granddaughter into her arms.

"It's so dark and I'm afraid," the girl sobbed, burrowing into the older woman's embrace. "Doesn't anything ever frighten you, Savta?" she cried. Mary smoothed the tousled hair, her heart aching for the orphaned child.

"Ah, yes my little one. I was once afraid of so many things." She closed her eyes, remembering. Then she smiled at the child in her arms. "Shall I tell you a wonderful story about how God showed me He was greater than my fear?"

Sarah wiped at her tears and nodded, eyes searching her grandmother's face.

Mary softly stroked the child's cheek. "Well, when I was just a young woman, my closest friend, whose name was also Mary, became very sick. She had fevers and terrifying visions that made her scream with fear. And then, one day, a teacher named Jesus touched her and she felt a warm and comforting light fill her heart, pushing out all the darkness and pain, healing her completely. From that moment, she left her family to follow Jesus, to serve Him, and to learn from Him. I knew that Jesus must be a prophet, sent from God; but I was afraid to go with her. So I didn't see my friend again for a long time. Then one spring, I went to Jerusalem to celebrate the Passover and I spied her, Mary of Magdalene, in the crowd. She ran to me and we embraced. She told me that something horrible had happened. The Roman governor, Pilate, had condemned Jesus to death on a cross! We were so sure Jesus was the Messiah, God's Chosen One. How could this be? Terrified, we followed the soldiers as they led Jesus to the hill called Golgotha and watched as they crucified Him between two thieves. We stood helpless, weeping; and then, right in the middle of the day, the sky became dark as night, the earth shook, Jesus cried out one more time, and then He died."

Sarah turned in her grandmother's arms. "But if He loved Jesus, why did God let Him die?"

"We asked ourselves that too: How could a caring Father take away the One we loved?"

"Like Mama?" Sarah whispered.

"Yes, my darling." She hugged the girl tightly, then continued. "But that dark moment was not the end of the story. Two men removed the body of Jesus from the cross, wrapped it tenderly in cloths, and laid it in a garden tomb. Then, for safekeeping, they rolled a huge stone in front of

Photograph © Jeff Kinsey/Shutterstock

the tomb. Mary Magdalene and I watched until they finished and then we ran away. For that whole long night and the next day, we hid, frightened, our hearts as dark as that tomb. But then, as the sun rose on the first day of the week, even though we were still afraid, we decided to act."

Sarah sat up now, eyes wide. "What did you do, Savta?"

"We ran back to the tomb. We had to be close to Jesus, even in death. As we came near, the earth shook, there was a thunderous sound, and we gasped at what we saw. The huge stone was rolled away and there, blazing with light, sat an angel dressed in shimmering white. 'Don't be afraid,' he said. 'Jesus is not here. He was raised from the dead. You must hurry and tell His friends!'"

"But how could He live again?" Sarah asked.

"We didn't know. It was impossible! But we ran to do what the angel said. And now here is the most amazing part of my story." Mary turned Sarah around and took the young girl's hands in her own. "This is why I no longer fear the dark. As we ran from the open tomb, Jesus appeared to us, standing right in our path, smiling and looking at us with such love. We fell to the ground and grasped His feet, worshiping Him. 'Don't be frightened,' He said. 'Go tell My brothers, then all of you come meet Me in Galilee. I am alive!' We could hardly believe our own ears and eyes. But it was all true. He did appear to us again. And He explained that the darkness we know here on earth is only a pass-

ing shadow. That He, the brightness of God, the brilliance of heaven, is always with us."

Sarah looked at her grandmother's hands, worn and wrinkled with age; then she gazed into the loving eyes she had known all her life. "Will Jesus always be here for me, Savta? Even when I cannot see Him?"

"Oh yes, my darling, always." Mary helped Sarah lie back down, tucking the worn blanket around her. Then into the stillness of the night she whispered a prayer: "Thank You, Lord, for keeping Your promise to vanquish our darkness with Your everlasting light."

On Easter Morn

Elizabeth Coatsworth

On Easter morn,
On Easter morn,
The sun comes dancing
    up the sky.

His light leaps up;
It shakes and swings,
Bewildering the dazzled eye.

On Easter morn
All earth is glad;
The waves rejoice in
    the bright sea.

Be still and listen
To your heart,
And hear it beating merrily.

FROM
The Morning Purples All the Sky

A. R. Thompson

The morning purples all the sky,
The air with praises rings;
Defeated hell stands sullen by,
The world exulting sings:
"Glory to God!" our glad lips cry;
"All praise and worship be
On earth, in heaven, to God Most High,
For Christ's great victory!"

Apple orchard near Winchester, Virginia.
Photograph © William H. Johnson

Smile Praises, O Sky!

Author Unknown
Translated by Elizabeth Charles

Smile praises, O sky!
Soft breathe them, O air!
Below and on high,
And everywhere.
The black troop of storms
Has yielded to calm;
Tufted blossoms are peeping,
And early palm.

Arouse thee, O spring!
Ye flowers, come forth,
With thousand hues tinting
The soft green earth;
Ye violets tender,
And sweet roses bright,
Gay Lent-lilies blended
With pure lilies white.

Sweep, tides of rich music,
The full veins along;
And pour in full measure,
Sweet lyres, your song.
Sing, sing, for He liveth—
He lives, as He said;
The Lord has arisen
Unharmed from the dead.

Clap, clap your hands, mountains!
Ye valleys, resound!
Leap, leap for joy, fountains!
Ye hills, catch the sound.
All triumph! He liveth—
He lives, as He said;
The Lord hath arisen
Unharmed from the dead.

Photograph © Jill Lang/Jilllang/Dreamstime.com

Easter Bells

Gladys Harp

Ring out the Easter bells to tell
That Christ, the Lord, has risen;
No tomb was ever strong enough
Our Savior to imprison.

Ring out the Easter bells to tell
That He who died to save,
And rose again on Easter morn
Has triumphed o'er the grave.

Ring out the Easter bells again
That none may fail to hear

The message that some gladsome morn
The Lord will reappear.

Ring out the happy Easter bells
That tell the story true
That on the Resurrection morn
All life is born anew.

Ring out the bells to tell again
Eternal life is given
To all we mortals who believe
That Christ, the Lord, is risen.

Easter Hymn

Henry Vaughan

Death and darkness, get you packing—
Nothing now to man is lacking;
All your triumphs now are ended,
And what Adam marred is mended;
Graves are beds now for the weary,
Death a nap, to wake more merry;
Youth now, full of pious duty,
Seeks in thee for perfect beauty;
The weak and aged, tired with length
Of days, from thee look for new strength;
And infants with thy pangs contest
As pleasant, as if with the breast.
Then, unto Him, who thus hath thrown
Even to contempt thy kingdom down,
And by His blood did us advance
Unto His own interitance,
To Him be glory, power, praise,
From this, unto the last of days!

Beautiful spring scene in Westfield, New Jersey.
Photograph © Gene Ahrens/Superstock

Eastertide

Gladys Harp

Little downy, yellow chicks,
Eggs of every hue,
Signifying this Eastertide
That life is born anew.

The resurrection of lost dreams,
Of flowers, leaves, and grass;

The end of strife, the dawn of peace,
That now has come to pass.

The joyous lift of love that sweeps
Across the countryside;
May all the joy of blessings now
Be yours this Eastertide.

ISBN-13: 978-0-8249-1339-7

Published by Ideals Publications, a Guideposts Company
Nashville, Tennessee
www.idealsbooks.com

Publisher, Peggy Schaefer
Editor, Melinda L. R. Rumbaugh
Copy Editor, Kaye Dacus
Designer, Marisa Jackson
Permissions Editor, Kristi West

Cover: Tulips and grape hyacinth, Keukenhof Gardens, Holland, Netherlands. Photograph © Radius/SuperStock
Inside front cover: *Daffodils and Primroses in a Basket* by Joan Thewsey. Image © Private Collection/The Bridgeman Art Library
Inside back cover: *Easter Basket, 1996* by Linda Benton. Image © Private Collection/The Bridgeman Art Library
Art for "Bits & Pieces" by Kathy Rusynyk. Feature logos and spot art for back cover, pages 1, 27, 36, 38, and 64 by Lisa Reed. Seamless damask pattern, pages 45, 46, and 49, copyright © thijsone/iStockphoto.com; vintage design elements pages 45, 46, and 49 © Antonova Olena/iStockphoto.com. "Beneath the Cross of Jesus" sheet music by Dick Torrans, Melode, Inc.

Readers are invited to submit original poetry and prose for possible use in future publications. Please send no more than four typed submissions to: Magazine Submis-sions, Ideals Publications, 2630 Elm Hill Pike, Suite 100, Nashville, Tennessee 37214. Manuscripts will be returned if a self-addressed stamped envelope is included.

ACKNOWLEDGMENTS:
ALDIS, DOROTHY. "When" from *All Together* by Dorothy Aldis, copyright 1925–1928, 1934, 1939, 1952, renewed 1953, © 1954–1956, 1962 by Dorothy Aldis, © by Roy E. Porter, renewed. Used by permission of G.P. Putnam's Sons, A Division of Penguin Young Readers Group. All rights reserved. COATSWORTH, ELIZABETH. "On Easter Morn." Reprinted by permission of The Marsh Agency Ltd. on behalf of the Estate of Elizabeth Coatsworth. FISHER, AILEEN. "Easter's Coming" from *Skip Around the Year* by Aileen Fisher. Copyright © 1967 Aileen Fisher. © Renewed 1995 Aileen Fisher. Used by permission of the Boulder Public Library Foundation, Inc. and Marian Reiner on their behalf. MCLOUGHLAND, BEVERLY. "In March." Copyright © 1987 Highlights for Children, Inc., Columbus, Ohio. Used by permission. UPDIKE, JOHN. Quote from *Self-Consciousness* by John Updike. Published by Random House, Inc. OUR THANKS to the following authors or their heirs: Michelle Medlock Adams, Ruth Carrington, Gerry Childs, Laurie E. Dawson, Joan Donaldson, Earle J. Grant, Edgar A. Guest, Gladys Harp, Clay Harrison, William D. Hicks, Martha Hood, Pamela Kennedy, LaVerne P. Larson, Marcia K. Leaser, Louisa Godissart McQuillen, Conny Manero, Virginia Blanck Moore, Kathleen R. Pawley, Sheila J. Petre, Irene Randol, Jane McGuire Reneau, Margaret Ann Rorke, Gail L. Roberson, Diane Skinner, Eileen Spinelli, Alice M. Stewart, William L. Stidger, Susan Sundwall, N. Anne Highlands Tiley, Ethel Wilson.

Scripture quotations marked RSV are taken from the Revised Standard Version of the Bible, copyright 1952 [2nd edition, 1971] by the Division of Christian Education of the National Council of the Churches of Christ in the United States of America. Used by permission. All rights reserved.

Every effort has been made to establish ownership and use of each selection in this book. If contacted, the publisher will be pleased to rectify any inadvertent errors or omissions in subsequent editions.

Easter Recipes from ideals®

This Easter season, enjoy and share these crowd-pleasing dishes with family and friends. Featured are three recipes for an Eastertime brunch, a simple dinner menu to serve before or after your family's Easter egg hunt, and four delicious desserts for any spring day. Any occasion will benefit from these handy recipe cards throughout this joy-filled time of year.

Easter Breakfast Casserole

1 16-ounce package frozen hash brown potatoes, thawed
2 tablespoons butter
   Salt and black pepper
3 cups shredded Cheddar cheese
1 pound bacon, cooked and crumbled
¼ cup diced onion
¼ cup diced green or red bell pepper
8 eggs
1½ cups milk

Preheat oven to 425°F. Spread hash browns in bottom of a greased 2-quart casserole dish. Dot with butter and sprinkle with salt and pepper to taste. Bake 30 minutes or until lightly browned. Remove from oven; reduce heat to 350°F. In a medium bowl, mix together cheese, bacon, onion, green pepper,

(Continued on back)

Fruit Salad with Lemon Poppy Seed Dressing

½ cup granulated sugar
½ cup lemon juice
2 teaspoons diced onion
1 teaspoon Dijon mustard
½ teaspoon salt
⅔ cup olive oil
1 tablespoon poppy seeds
1 head romaine lettuce, torn into bite-sized pieces
4 ounces shredded Swiss cheese
1 cup cashews
½ cup dried cranberries
1 apple, peeled, cored, and diced
1 pear, peeled, cored, and diced

In a blender, combine sugar, lemon juice, onion, mustard, and salt. Add oil in a steady stream, blending until mixture is thick and smooth. Add poppy seeds and continue

(Continued on back)

Honey-Ricotta Turnovers

¾ cup whole-milk ricotta
3 tablespoons sugar
¼ teaspoon vanilla extract
1 teaspoon lemon or orange zest, optional
1 egg
   Coarse salt
¼ cup unsalted butter
2 tablespoons honey, plus more for serving
1 sheet frozen puff pastry, defrosted

Preheat oven to 350°F. In a small bowl, combine ricotta, sugar, vanilla, zest (if desired), egg, and pinch of salt. Mix well to combine. In a microwave-safe bowl, microwave butter and honey on high until butter melts, 30 to 45 seconds. Stir well to combine. Unfold puff pastry sheet and cut into thirds. Roll out lightly on floured board. Cut each piece into thirds (for

(Continued on back)

and salt and pepper to taste. In a large bowl, combine eggs and milk. Stir in cheese mixture and pour over baked hash browns. Cover with foil and bake 40 minutes. Remove foil and bake uncovered an additional 15 to 30 minutes, until the eggs have set. *Makes 12 servings.*

blending for a few more seconds; set aside. In a large bowl, combine lettuce, cheese, cashews, cranberries, apple, and pear; toss. Just before serving, pour dressing sparingly over salad; toss to coat. Refrigerate remaining dressing or serve alongside salad. *Makes 12 servings.*

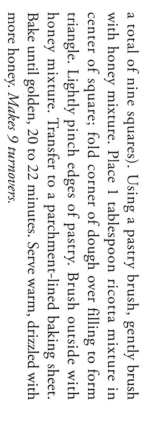

a total of nine squares). Using a pastry brush, gently brush with honey mixture. Place 1 tablespoon ricotta mixture in center of square; fold corner of dough over filling to form triangle. Lightly pinch edges of pastry. Brush outside with honey mixture. Transfer to a parchment-lined baking sheet. Bake until golden, 20 to 22 minutes. Serve warm, drizzled with more honey. *Makes 9 turnovers.*

Sweet Green Bean Bundles

1 pound fresh green beans, ends trimmed
½ pound bacon strips, cut in half
⅓ cup butter, melted
⅔ cup brown sugar
1 teaspoon garlic salt

Preheat oven to 350°F. Blanch green beans in boiling water for 1½ to 2 minutes. Quickly immerse in a cold water bath; remove and dry on paper towels. Gather 7 green beans into bundle and wrap with half-strip of bacon; repeat for remaining beans. Place in a 9 x 13-inch baking dish. In a small bowl, combine butter and brown sugar. Pour evenly over green bean bundles. Sprinkle garlic salt on top. Bake, uncovered, 30 minutes or until bacon is browned, occasionally glazing with butter mixture. *Makes 8 servings of 2 bundles each.*

Pear Roquefort Salad

1 head romaine lettuce, torn in bite-sized pieces
½ cup pecan halves
⅓ cup olive oil
3 tablespoons red wine vinegar
1½ teaspoons prepared mustard
1 clove garlic, chopped
½ teaspoon salt
Black pepper to taste
¼ cup plus 1½ teaspoons granulated sugar, divided
3 pears, peeled, cored, and chopped
5 ounces Roquefort cheese, crumbled
½ cup thinly sliced green onion
1 avocado, peeled, pitted, and diced

In a skillet over medium heat, combine ¼ cup sugar and pecans, stirring frequently, until the sugar has melted and caramelized the pecans. Carefully spread pecans onto

(Continued on back)

Prime Rib Roast

1 6- to 7-pound prime rib roast
7 cloves garlic, minced
1½ tablespoons olive oil
1 teaspoon salt
1 teaspoon black pepper
1 teaspoon dried thyme

Allow roast to sit out 30 to 45 minutes to bring to room temperature before cooking.

Preheat oven to 400°F. Place beef in roasting pan with bone side down. In a small bowl, mix garlic, olive oil, salt, pepper, and thyme. Spread mixture over the top and sides of roast; cook 20 minutes. Reduce heat to 325°F and cook an additional 1¾ to 2¼ hours until a meat thermometer measures an internal temperature of 125°F for medium rare. (Begin checking temperature at 1½ hours to avoid overcooking.)

(Continued on back)

Sweet Potato Soufflé

3 large sweet potatoes (enough to make 3 cups mashed), peeled and cubed
Salt
¾ cup granulated sugar
⅓ cup butter, softened
2 eggs, beaten
1 teaspoon vanilla extract
½ cup milk
1 cup shredded coconut
⅓ cup all-purpose flour
1 cup brown sugar
1 cup chopped walnuts
⅓ cup butter, melted

Place potatoes in a large pot; add cold water to cover by 1 inch. Add 1 tablespoon salt for every quart of water. Bring to a boil; cover and boil until a fork can easily pierce to the center, about 15 to 25 minutes. Drain; let cool enough to safely handle. Mash and reserve 3 cups for recipe. Preheat oven to 350°F.

(Continued on back)

Check every 15 minutes until desired temperature is achieved.) Baste meat once or twice with drippings during roasting time. Remove from oven and allow to rest for 20 minutes before carving. *Makes 6 to 8 servings.*

waxed paper. Cool and break into pieces. In a small bowl, blend oil, vinegar, 1½ teaspoons sugar, mustard, garlic, salt, and pepper; set aside. In a large serving bowl, layer lettuce, pears, cheese, onion, and avocado. Just before serving, pour dressing over salad. Sprinkle with pecans and serve. *Makes 6 servings.*

In a large bowl, mix sweet potatoes, granulated sugar, ½ cup butter, eggs, vanilla, and milk. Pour into a 2-quart baking dish. In a medium bowl, combine coconut, flour, brown sugar, walnuts, and ⅓ cup melted butter. Sprinkle mixture over sweet potatoes. Bake 30 to 35 minutes. *Makes 8 to 10 servings.*

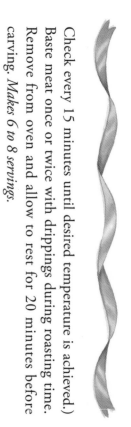

Fresh Strawberry Pie

1 refrigerated pie crust
1½ quarts (about 6 cups) strawberries, hulled and halved
1 cup granulated sugar
2 tablespoons cornstarch
Red food coloring, optional
1 3-ounce package cream cheese, softened
1 teaspoon grated lemon peel

Bring crust to room temperature per package instructions and gently unroll crust. Preheat oven to 450°F. Fold pie crust into fourths; place in 9-inch glass pie plate. Unfold and ease into plate, pressing firmly against bottom and side. Fold excess crust under itself over rim and press together to form thick edge. Prick bottom and side with fork. Bake 10 to 12 minutes or until light brown. Cool on cooling rack.

(Continued on back)

Angel Food Delight

1 8-ounce package cream cheese, softened
2 cups frozen whipped topping, thawed, divided
1 8-ounce can crushed pineapple in juice
1 3.4-ounce package cheesecake-flavored instant pudding mix
1 prepared angel food cake
10 whole strawberries

In a medium bowl, combine cream cheese, 1 cup whipped topping, pineapple with juice, and pudding mix; mix well. Cut angel food cake horizontally into 3 layers. Place bottom layer on a serving plate. Spread 1 cup pineapple mixture over bottom layer. Top with second layer and cover layer with 1 cup pineapple mixture. Place third layer on top and spread

(Continued on back)

Italian Coconut Cake

2 cups all-purpose flour
1 teaspoon baking soda
⅛ teaspoon salt
2 cups granulated sugar
1¼ cups butter, softened, divided
5 eggs, separated
1 cup buttermilk
1 teaspoon vanilla extract
3 cups sweetened flaked coconut, divided
¾ cup pecans, chopped
1 8-ounce package cream cheese, softened
1 1-pound box confectioners' sugar

Preheat oven to 350°F. In a medium bowl, sift together flour, baking soda, and salt; set aside. In a large bowl, cream sugar and 1 cup butter. Stir in egg yolks, buttermilk, and vanilla; mix well. Gradually add flour mixture, stirring after each addition. Add 2 cups coconut and ½ cup chopped pecans. In a

(Continued on back)

Carrot-Cake Cheesecake Bars

1 15- to 18-ounce box carrot cake mix
3 eggs
½ cup butter, softened
2 8-ounce packages cream cheese, softened
1 teaspoon vanilla extract
½ cup granulated sugar
1 cup prepared cream-cheese frosting, optional

Preheat oven to 350°F. In a large bowl, stir together cake mix, 1 egg, and butter, mixing to form thick dough. Press dough into a greased 9 x 13-inch pan; set aside. In a medium bowl, beat cream cheese until smooth. Beat in remaining 2 eggs and vanilla; add sugar and continue beating until creamy and smooth. Pour over the carrot cake dough in the pan. Bake 30 to 40

(Continued on back)

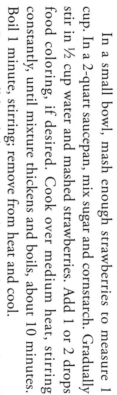

In a small bowl, mash enough strawberries to measure 1 cup. In a 2-quart saucepan, mix sugar and cornstarch. Gradually stir in ½ cup water and mashed strawberries. Add 1 or 2 drops food coloring, if desired. Cook over medium heat, stirring constantly, until mixture thickens and boils, about 10 minutes. Boil 1 minute, stirring; remove from heat and cool.

In a small bowl, beat cream cheese and lemon peel until well incorporated; spread evenly in bottom of crust. Evenly distribute remaining strawberry halves. Pour cooked strawberry mixture over top. Chill until set, about 3 hours. Store in refrigerator. *Makes 8 servings.*

remaining pineapple mixture on top of cake. Cover sides with remaining 1 cup whipped topping. Just before serving, top with fresh strawberries. *Makes 12 servings.*

separate bowl, beat egg whites until stiff peaks form. Gently fold into batter. Divide batter into 3 lightly greased and floured 9-inch round cake pans. Bake 30 minutes; allow to cool.

In a medium bowl, mix together cream cheese and ¼ cup butter. Gradually add confectioners' sugar until frosting is of desired consistency. Place bottom cake layer on a serving plate; spread frosting on top. Place second layer over bottom layer and frost top. Top with third layer and frost top and sides of all layers. Sprinkle remaining coconut and pecans over top of cake, if desired. *Makes 12 servings.*

minutes or until the edges start to pull away from the pan. Cool completely in pan on cooling rack.

Cut into bars and drop a dollop of frosting on each bar, if desired. *Makes about 2 dozen bars.*